Sharks: 100 Amazing Pictures
Never Known Befor

By Bandana Ojha

All Rights Reserved ©2020

Introduction

Filled with up-to-date information, color photos, fascinating & fun facts this book " Sharks:100 Amazing Fun Facts with Pictures " is the best book for kids to find out more about the amazing ocean creature Shark .This book would definitely satisfy the children's curiosity and help them to understand why sharks are special—and what makes them different from other sea creatures .The book gives a story, history, detailed science, explores the interesting and amazing fun facts about sharks. It's a fun and fascinating way for young readers to find out more about the world's dangerous bull shark, the feared great white shark, fastest Mako shark, the fanged nurse shark, cutest zebra shark, the largest and gentle whale shark, second largest basking shark, the carpet shark Wobbegong and many more. All about the smallest, cutest, Fastest, largest, how they communicate, when they discovered, information about their strongest jaws, teeth, their brain, eyes, ears, scales, skin- all bits of information which can touch the kid's inquisitive mind. With its awesome facts and action-packed images, this book brings kids close to the mysterious lives of sharks. This is a great chance for every kid to expand their knowledge about sharks and impress family and friends with all discovered and never known before fun filled facts.

1. Sharks have been around for about 400 million years. They are the top predators of the ocean's natural food chain.

2. Sharks live in every ocean on the planet.

3. There are more than 470 species of sharks split across thirteen orders, including four orders of sharks that have gone extinct.

4. Sharks belong to the class of fish, Chondrichthyes.

5. Each type of shark has a different shaped tooth depending on their diet.

6. Almost all sharks are "carnivores" or meat eaters. They live on a diet of fish and sea mammals (like dolphins and seals) and even such prey as turtles and seagulls.

7. Sharks even eat other sharks. For example, a tiger shark might eat a bull shark, a bull shark might eat a blacktip shark and a blacktip shark might eat a dogfish shark!

8. The size of a shark species relates to where they hunt. Smaller sharks tend to feed near the ocean floor. Larger sharks hunt in the middle depths and near the surface

where they can more easily snatch larger prey such as seals.

9. Sharks' skeletons are made entirely of cartilage, an elastic tissue that is much softer than bones. When a shark dies, salt from the ocean water completely dissolves its skeleton, leaving only the sharks teeth behind.

10. Unlike fish, sharks can only swim forward. That is because their fins are stiff and cannot be controlled by muscles.

11. Another thing that makes sharks different from fish is their scales. Sharks have dermal denticles also called placoid scales, which are smooth and help them move quickly through the water. Fish have flat, rough scales.

12. Unlike most fish, sharks don't have a gas-filled swim bladder. Instead, they have an oil filled liver that offers buoyancy, using this in conjunction with forward movement to control vertical position.

13. Sharks have the most powerful jaws on the planet. Unlike most animals' jaws, both the sharks' upper and lower jaws move.

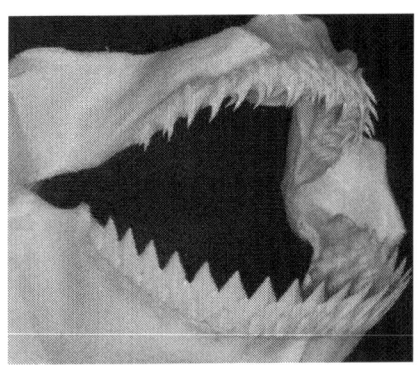

14. An average shark has 40-45 teeth in up to seven rows. Sharks lose teeth regularly and can go through 30,000 teeth in their lifetime.

15. Most sharks are "cold-blooded" or more precisely, poikilothermic. This means that their internal body temperature matches that of their surrounding environment.

16. A shark bites with its lower jaw first and then its upper. It tosses its head back and forth to tear loose a piece of meat which it swallows whole.

17. Sharks move like airplanes! A shark creates forward movement by moving its tail, which acts like a propeller. As the shark

moves forward, water moves over its fins as though they were wings, creating lift.

18. Even though sharks have rows and rows of razor-sharp teeth, they don't use them to chew their prey. Shark teeth are strictly for snapping, gripping, crushing or ripping, and the resulting chunks are swallowed whole.

19. Sharks have an astounding array of senses, including the sense of smell, sight, hearing and picking up vibrations. Their sense of smell is so powerful that they can detect a single drop of blood in an Olympic-sized pool.

20. Sharks can use the heartbeat of their prey to track them. Sharks have special sensing organs called ampullae of Lorenzini and they use this to detect electromagnetic fields which all living creatures emit.

21. The smallest shark in the world is the Dwarf Lantern Shark (Etmopterus perryi). A fully-grown Dwarf Lantern Shark can measure to a maximum of 20cm.

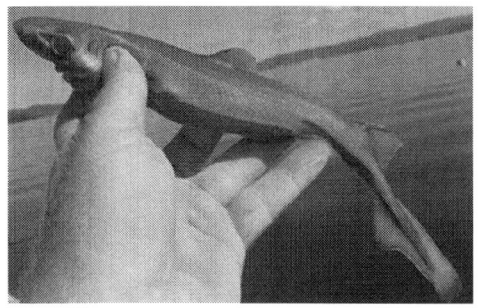

22. The oldest known species of living shark is the goblin shark that has been around for 120 million years. The second oldest is the

frilled shark that has been around for 80 million years.

23. Great whites can jump out of the water up to ten feet to catch their prey. This is done to beat the competition for food.

24. Great white sharks can be found throughout the world's oceans, mostly in cool waters close to the coast.

25. Great white sharks are grey with a white underbelly, from where they get their name. They have a streamlined shape and powerful tails that propel them through the water at over 60km per hour.

26. Great white sharks eat an average of 11 tons of food a year. They can live up to 3 months without eating.

27. Great white sharks can weigh up to 5,000 pounds.

28. Sharks sometimes act as scavengers and will often feed on dead animals such as whales. This is how sharks help keep our oceans healthy and marine life in check.

29. Sharks help to make sure that reefs are protected from other predators to ensure the reef, and all the fish that live on and around the reef, thrive as an important ecosystem.

30. A shark's tooth-shaped skin, called denticles, allow it to move swiftly through the water without collecting barnacles and algae deposits on it.

31. Most sharks species will drown if they stop moving. Examples are great white, Mako and salmon sharks - they don't have the muscles they need to pump water through their mouth and over their gills.

32. Sharks have a lateral line organ which acts like an internal barometer. When solid objects glide through the water, they create waves of pressure. By sensing these pressure waves, a shark can detect both the movement and direction of any object or fish.

33. The most dangerous sharks are the Great White shark, the Tiger shark, the Hammerhead shark, the Mako shark and the Bull shark.

34. Not all sharks are dangerous. The most harmless sharks tend to be the largest! The basking shark, the whale shark and the megamouth sharks all fit this description.

35. Sharks have a highly evolved sense of hearing, which allows them to hear low-frequency sounds from up to quarter mile away.

36. Sharks' eyes are on the sides of their heads, so they have an amazingly wide sightline spanning nearly 360 degrees. Their panoramic view of the undersea world is inhibited only by two blind spots: one in front of the snout and the other directly behind the tail.

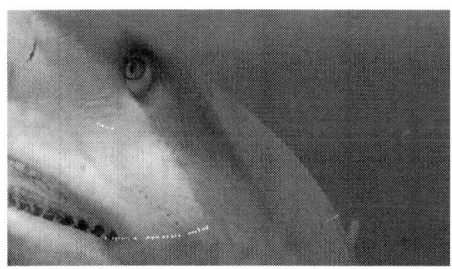

37. The largest living shark in the world is the Whale Shark. These Sharks grow to lengths of around 12-14 meters and weigh over 21 tons.

38. ZEBRA SHARK is the small and gentle shark that can be kept in an aquarium with other fish. Its tail is half its length.

39. Wobbegong Sharks possibly have the best camouflage of all sharks. Their symmetrical pattern of bold markings resembles a carpet. Because of this striking

pattern, wobbegongs are often referred to as carpet sharks.

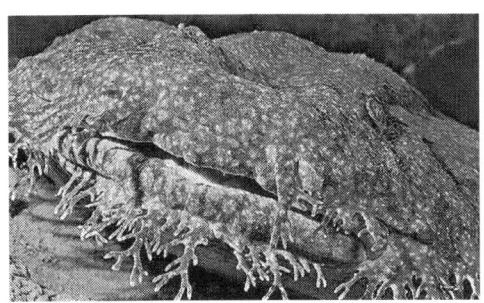

40. The fastest shark in the world is none other than the short fin Mako shark. The Mako is capable of bursts of speed up to 18.8 meters per second or 68-70 kilometers per hour.

41. The world's second largest living shark can be found around the UK and Ireland, the Basking Shark (about 30 feet long and 8,000 pounds).

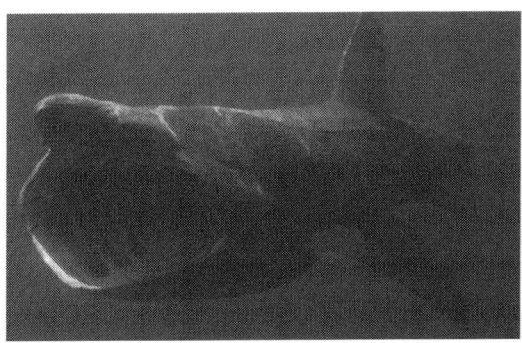

42. GREAT WHITE SHARK attack more on people than any other type. Their averages length is 12 feet and average weight is 3,000 pounds. Unlike most sharks, it can lift its head out of the water.

43. The Whale Shark is so far the deepest diving recorded shark. One shark was measured down to a depth of around 1,800 meters below the ocean surface, almost two kilometers.

44. The jaws of sharks are not attached to their skull. They move separately, allowing them to thrust forward and latch onto prey.

45. The surface of a shark's jaws have extra support called 'tesserae'.

These tiny hexagonal plates are made up of calcium salt deposits, giving cartilage more strength.

46. Shark's may have up to 3,000 teeth at one time. They are fully embedded into the gums, with shape and size varying depending on their purpose.

47. Sharks continuously grow multiple rows of teeth. When a shark breaks or loses a tooth, a new one moves forward to replace it, much like a conveyor belt.

48. It's estimated that some sharks may lose 30,000 or more teeth in their lifetime. Tooth replacement rates vary from several days to several months.

49. Sharks eyes are located on the sides of their heads to give them a wider view of their surroundings.

50. Some sharks living in frigid waters can heat their eyes with a special organ in their eye socket, so they can hunt more efficiently regardless of the temperatures.

51. Sharks living deep in the water tend to have light color eyes to help them attract more light, while sharks living closer to the surface have darker colored eyes to shield them from the light.

52. Sharks communicate through body language. Some common communications involve zigzag swimming, head shaking, hunched backs, and head butts.

53. Sharks do not have vocal cords, so they make no sounds. That is why they are known as the "silent killers."

54. Sharks can have from 1 to 100 babies at a time, depending on the type of shark. The ones with pups that grow inside the mother have fewer babies at a time than sharks that lay eggs outside the body.

55. One of the reasons that sharks are such successful predators is that they have such super senses.

56. Sharks have the largest brains of any fish.

57. Two-thirds of a shark's brain is dedicated to its keenest sense -- smell.

58. There are several "shark" looking animals in the ocean that are rays, not sharks. Examples are the Guitar fish and the

Bow Mouth Ray. Often these rays are called sharks incorrectly.

59. It's a shark eat shark world! Sometimes even before the sharks are born. When some species' embryos begin to develop teeth, they eat their unborn siblings until one shark remains, an act known as intrauterine cannibalism.

60. Sharks such as the Great White and Mako sharks are homeothermic and maintain a higher body temperature than the

surrounding water. Muscles in the center of the body provides extra heat for bursts of speed when hunting

61. Angel sharks can ambush their prey in one-tenth of one second.

62. The thresher shark has a tail that can grow to about half its body length. They use their tails to slap their prey to death.

63. Bamboo sharks don't swim. They use four different fins to walk across the ocean floor.

64. Lantern sharks use bioluminescence making them glow in the dark. They use this trick to attract mates and confuse their prey.

65. The bull shark can survive in freshwater.

66. The epaulette shark can use its fins like legs, to walk, when the tide is too low to swim.

67. Possibly one of the most evolved sharks today are hammerhead sharks. They have an advanced sensory system and a body shape that has adapted to hunt specific prey.

68. Nurse Shark is known as bottom dwelling shark. It has a thin, fleshy, whisker-like organs on the lower jaw in front of the nostrils that they use to touch and taste.

69. The Goblin Shark has the reputation of being the ugliest shark in the world. They

are a rare deep-water species that have an extending jaw to snap and capture prey in the ocean's depths.

70. The megamouth shark is a species of deep-water shark. It is rarely seen by humans and is the smallest of the three filter feeding sharks alongside the whale shark and basking shark.

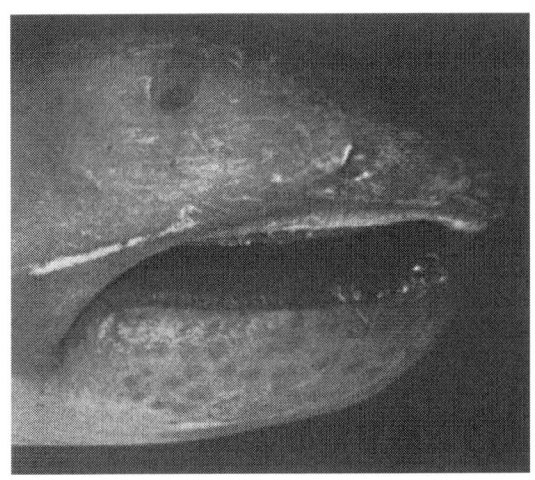

71. The Greenland shark also known as the gurry shark or grey shark, is a large shark of the family Somniosidae ("sleeper sharks"), closely related to the Pacific and southern sleeper sharks.

72. The grey shark has the longest known lifespan of all vertebrate species (estimated to be between 300–500 years) and is among the largest extant species of shark.

73. Depending on the species, sharks display three ways to bear their young:

Oviparity = laying eggs

viviparity = born alive & functional

ovoviviparity = Eggs hatch inside the adult female and sharks are born alive.

74. Sharks need to keep moving to breathe. Some species have evolved to remain stationary, resting on the sea bed and pumping water over their gills.

75. Shark anatomy is consistent across the species. But each have their own unique features.

76. Sharks can store food in their stomachs for months.

77. Sharks rely on electroreception to navigate the ocean and notice prey.

78. When a great white shark is born, along with up to a dozen siblings, it immediately swims away from its mother. Baby sharks are on their own right from the start, and their mother may see them only as prey.

79. Age of a shark can be measured by counting the rings on its vertebrae.

80. A membrane in the back of the eye called the tapetum lucidum reflects sunlight back into the eye, so the shark can make more use of what little light is there.

81. Most female sharks will lose their appetites before giving birth. This is a biologically trigger to prevent them from eating their own pups.

82. While most sharks prefer to hunt alone, there are some species of shark – such as the Blue shark or the Scalloped Hammerhead, that can be found hunting in groups known as "schools," and often travel great distances this way as well.

83. When a shark eats food that it can't digest (like a turtle shell or tin can), it can vomit by thrusting its stomach out its mouth then pulling it back in.

84. The Grey Reef shark has been called the "gangster shark" because of its highly aggressive nature.

85. Angel sharks were once called monkfish or bishop fish because their fins look like flowing robes.

86. The world's most unusual shark, the megamouth shark, mouth can reach up to three feet across, while the rest of the body is about 16 feet long.

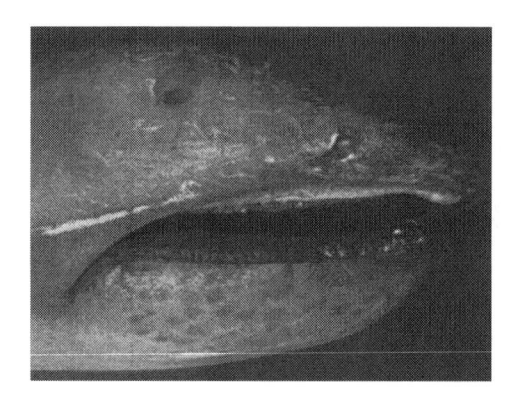

87. Some sharks can bite hard enough to cut through a thick piece of steel. Like lions and other predators, sharks usually kill only when they are hungry, which isn't very

often. Some sharks can live a year without eating, living off the oil they stored in their bodies.

88. The second-most dangerous shark in the world, the tiger shark, is sometimes called the "garbage can of the sea" because it will eat anything, including animal carcasses, tin cans, car tires, and other garbage. One was even found having a chicken coop with the remains of bones and feathers inside its stomach.

89. 97 % of all sharks are completely harmless to humans. This is due to their size and teeth design. Most shark teeth are not designed for large prey. These sharks stick to small prey like fish, crustaceans or cephalopods.

90. Sharks DO NOT EAT human. Sharks are attracted to their natural prey. When sharks meet humans, it is usually by mistaken identity or the shark was in search of its food.

91. Sharks sometimes act as scavengers and will often feed on dead animals such as

whales. This is how sharks help keep our oceans healthy and marine life in check.

92. Sharks help to make sure that reefs are protected from other predators to ensure the reef, and all the fish that live on and around the reef, thrive as an important ecosystem.

93. More than 90% of shark attacks (even from Great White Sharks) on humans are NON-FATAL. Once the shark realized it mis-identified a human for its normal natural prey, such as seals or a turtle, the shark lost interest and swam away.

94. Shark attacks are extremely rare and account for four fatalities every single year worldwide.

95. Sharks have few natural predators. Killer whales, seals, crocodiles, and larger sharks will eat sharks. The biggest threat to sharks is humans.

Killer Whale

96. Unfortunately due to overfishing and shark finning, some populations of certain shark species have been hunted down by approximately 90%.

97. According to the Shark Project, an estimated 200 million sharks are killed each year by humans, all for different purposes, such as meat, leather, and even demand for their teeth and dorsal fins.

98. Weird things that have been found in shark stomachs include shoes, chairs, a box of nails, a torpedo, drums, and bottles.

99. Marine debris, especially plastic, is extremely dangerous for sharks, whales and turtles. These creatures often end up ingesting plastic items which will eventually be fatal.

100. One of the best ways that a person can help in their own home to save Sharks is to

recycle as much plastic as possible that might otherwise end up in the ocean.

Please check this out:

Our other best-selling books for kids are-

My First Fruits

Most Popular Animal Quiz book for Kids: 100 amazing animal facts

Quiz Book for Kids: Science, History, Geography, Biology, Computer & Information Technology

English Grammar for Kids: Most Easy Way to learn English Grammar

Solar System & Space Science- Quiz for Kids: What You Know About Solar System

Know about Sharks: 100 Amazing Fun Facts with Pictures

Know About Whales:100+ Amazing & Interesting Fun Facts with Pictures: " Never known Before "- Whales facts

Know About Dinosaurs: 100 Amazing & Interesting Fun Facts with Pictures

Know About Kangaroos: Amazing & Interesting Facts with Pictures

Know About Penguins: 100+ Amazing Penguin Facts with Pictures

Know About Dolphins :100 Amazing Dolphin Facts with Pictures

100 Amazing Quiz Q & A About Penguin: Never Known Before Penguin Facts

English Grammar Practice Book for elementary kids: 1000+ Practice Questions with Answers

A to Z of English Tense

All About New York: 100+ Amazing Facts with Pictures

All About New Jersey: 100+ Amazing Facts with Pictures

All About California: 100+ Amazing Facts with Pictures

All About Arizona: 100+ Amazing Facts with Pictures